JOB

THE PATIENT FRIEND

TOLD BY CARINE MACKENZIE
ILLUSTRATIONS BY FRED APPS

10 9 8 7 6 5 4 3 2 1
Copyright © 2014 Carine Mackenzie
Published by Christian Focus Publications, Geanies House,
Fearn, Tain, Ross-shire, IV20 1TW, Scotland, U.K.
Printed in China.
ISBN: 978-1-78191-327-7
www.christianfocus.com

CF4•K

Job lived in the land of Uz. He was a good man who feared God.

He had a wife and a grown-up family of seven sons and three daughters.

Job was a wealthy man – he had 7,000 sheep, 3,000 camels, 500 pairs of oxen, 500 donkeys and a large house with many servants.

Job's children had homes of their own and often met for a meal together. Job had a concern for his children and would regularly offer sacrifices to God for them, praying that God would forgive their sins.

God was pleased with how Job respected him and avoided evil. Satan, the evil one, also noticed how Job lived. 'Job is only good because he has an easy life and plenty of possessions,' he said to God. 'Take that away and he would curse you.'

So God allowed Satan to test Job's faith by attacking his possessions.

One day a messenger came to Job with terrible news. 'The oxen were ploughing, the donkeys grazing beside them, when robbers came and took them away. I am the only farm hand to escape.'

Another came. 'Fire fell from heaven and burnt up all your sheep. I am the only shepherd to escape.'

Before that message was finished, another man rushed in. 'Raiders have taken all your camels and killed your servants. Only I have escaped.'

What devastating news for Job.

Then came even worse news. 'Your children were in their oldest brother's house. A great wind blew in from the desert and struck the house so it fell on them. They are all dead.'

Job was grief-stricken at this news, but he did not complain to God. He worshipped him.

'I was born with nothing and I shall die with nothing,' he said. 'The Lord gave me everything I have. They were his to take away. Blessed be the name of the Lord.'

Satan challenged God again. 'Job would not be so faithful if his body was suffering – then he would curse you.'

So God permitted Satan to attack Job's health, but insisted that his life must be spared.

Job's body broke out in painful boils from head to toe. He was miserable. He sat in a pile of ashes, scraping his sores with a piece of broken pottery.

Job's wife was no help to him. She urged him to curse God and die. Job refused.

'Don't speak so foolishly,' he said. 'We accept good things from God. Should we not accept the hard times too?'

Job reacted to his hard situation with grace and patience.

Job's three friends, Eliphaz, Bildad and Zophar came to comfort Job in his troubles. They wept, tore their robes and put dust on their heads to express their grief. For seven days and nights no one spoke a word.

Then, one by one, they offered well-meaning advice to Job. 'Man is born to trouble,' said Eliphaz. 'You deserve far worse,' said Zophar.

'God punishes the wicked,' Bildad added.

These men were good, religious men who made wonderful speeches, trying to bring comfort to Job, but they just made him feel worse.

Job was very depressed and upset by all that had happened, but he reacted to his friends' speeches with grace and wisdom.

'No matter what happens, I will still trust in God,' declared Job.

'You are all miserable comforters,' he said to his friends.

Job felt everyone was against him – his wife, his brothers, his friends; even little children despised him.

But through all this suffering, Job trusted in God. 'I know that my Redeemer lives,' he said, 'and that he will stand on the earth at last.'

Job was looking by faith to the Saviour, the Lord Jesus Christ. He believed in the resurrection of Jesus, God's Son and in the resurrection of God's people. He had the glorious hope that one day his perfected body would see God for himself.

'God knows what is happening to me and at the end of this trial, he will pronounce me as pure as gold.'

Then along came a younger man, Elihu. He was angry with Job's three friends because they had found no answer to Job's situation. 'I waited till now to speak,' he said, 'because I am younger than you.' That sounded very humble, but Elihu was far from humble.

He was angry with Job too and went on and on at great length, expressing his opinion about Job and about God and his justice and might.

He was no comfort at all to poor Job, accusing him of being an evil man. Elihu was convinced he was right and that he knew it all. Not a humble man at all.

Only when God spoke from a whirlwind did Job get a true picture of his suffering. His attention was directed to God's great power over the whole universe. God created the universe in the beginning and directs it day by day. The dawning of the day, the drops of rain, the thunder and lightning flash and every animal are all under God's direction.

Job was lost for words. 'I am of little importance. I can say nothing. I just put my hand over my mouth.'

Job realised that God does all things wisely. He knew then that his suffering was all in God's purpose and plan.

He confessed that he had said things that he should not have said, and thought things that were unwise.

He had heard about God previously, but now he knew him for himself.

Job repented of his sin.

God instructed Eliphaz, Zophar and Bildad to take seven bulls and seven rams and offer a sacrifice to God. 'My servant Job will pray for you,' said God. 'I will accept his prayer not to deal with you as your folly deserves. You have sinned in the way you spoke about my servant Job.'

Job received relief from his troubles when he prayed for his friends. The Lord heard his prayer.

God restored all his losses – in fact he gave him twice as much as he had before.

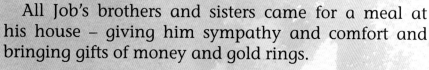

All Job's brothers and sisters came for a meal at his house – giving him sympathy and comfort and bringing gifts of money and gold rings.

Job received great blessings from God – twice as many sheep, camels, oxen and donkeys. He had seven more

sons and three more daughters. The girls, Jemimah, Keziah and Keren-Happuch were the most beautiful women in the land.

Job lived for 140 years after this, enjoying his children, grandchildren and great-grandchildren. The Lord greatly blessed him.

Job trusted in God and waited patiently for God to deliver him from his hard situation. He lost his family, his property and his health, but he did not complain or blame God. Trusting in God made a huge difference in Job's life.

When we trust in the Lord Jesus Christ as our Friend and Redeemer, that makes a big difference in the way we live too.

One of the results is patience, to look beyond our problems and to realise that the grace of God gives us all we need for every day.

The best thing God gives us is the forgiveness of sin through Jesus Christ, who gave his life so that those who trust in him would have eternal life.

Christ's death was not the end. It was part of God the Father's plan to save sinners. Christ's resurrection was another part of the plan – a plan which means that all who are brought to trust in Christ will also be raised to eternal life one day.

Job believed that his God would save him and redeem him and that one day he would see him in the flesh. 'I shall see him for myself,' he said.

All those who trust in the Lord Jesus Christ will see him in the flesh one day when he returns again to this earth, victorious.

What a wonderful, merciful, gracious God we have.